WORLD COMMODITIES

Coal

GARRY CHAPMAN » GARY HODGES

This edition first published in 2011 in the United States of America by Smart Apple Media.

Smart Apple Media
P.O. Box 3263
Mankato, MN, 56002

First published in 2010 by
MACMILLAN EDUCATION AUSTRALIA PTY LTD
15–19 Claremont Street, South Yarra 3141

Visit our web site at www.macmillan.com.au or go directly to www.macmillanlibrary.com.au

Associated companies and representatives throughout the world.

Copyright © Garry Chapman and Gary Hodges 2010

Library of Congress Cataloging-in-Publication Data

Chapman, Garry.
  Coal / Garry Chapman and Gary Hodges.
      p. cm. — (World commodities)
  Includes index.
  ISBN 978-1-59920-583-0 (library binding)
  1. Coal trade—Juvenile literature. 2. Coal—Juvenile literature. I. Hodges, Gary. II. Title.
  HD9540.5.C345 2011
  338.2'724—dc22
                                2010007304

Publisher: Carmel Heron
Commissioning Editor: Niki Horin
Managing Editor: Vanessa Lanaway
Editor: Laura Jeanne Gobal
Proofreader: Kirstie Innes-Will

Designer: Ivan Finnegan (cover and text)
Page Layout: Ivan Finnegan
Photo Researcher: Lesya Bryndzia (management: Debbie Gallagher)
Illustrators: Andy Craig and Nives Porcellato, **15**; Alan Laver, **17**, **19**, **28**, **29**

Manufactured in the United States of America by Corporate Graphics, Minnesota.
052010

Acknowledgments
The author and the publisher are grateful to the following for permission to reproduce copyright material:

Front cover photograph of coal: Mike and Jane Pelusey

Bloomberg via Getty Images/Alex Kraus, **12** (centre); Corbis/Nathan Benn, **25**, /EPA/Roland Weihrauch, **13** (middle), /Hulton-Deutsch Collection, **9** (top), /Chris Sattlberger, **10** (top), /Science Faction/Karen Kasmauski, **23**, /Xinhua Press/Hou Jun, **18**; Gebr. Eickhoff, **11** (bottom); Getty Images/AFP/Frederic J. Brown, **5**, /AFP/Kristian Buus, **21**, /AFP/Saul Loeb, **12** (bottom right), /Dorling Kindersley, **4** (iron ore), /Jeff J Mitchell, **22**, /National Geographic/Melissa Farlow, **27**, /Spencer Platt, **11** (2nd bottom), /Popperfoto/Rolls Press, **24**, /Jeff Smith, **10** (bottom); iStockphoto/Phil Augustavo, **11** (top); www.mountainroadshow.com, **11** (2nd top); Photolibrary/Glow Images, **13** (bottom), /Roel Loopers, **13** (top), /Photo Researchers, **12** (left), /SPL/Colin Cuthbert, **12** (top); Shutterstock/Forest Badger, **4** (oil), /Gtibbetts, **8**, /IDAL, **4** (wheat), /Ben Jeayes, **7**, /Brad Sauter, **14**, /GM Vozd, **9** (bottom), /WDG Photo, **26**, /Worldpics, **4** (coal), /yykkaa, **4** (sugar), /Magdalena Zurawska, **4** (coffee); UN Photo/Mark Garten, **20**.

While every care has been taken to trace and acknowledge copyright, the publisher tenders their apologies for any accidental infringement where copyright has proved untraceable. Where the attempt has been unsuccessful, the publisher welcomes information that would redress the situation.

Please note: At the time of printing, the Internet addresses appearing in this book were correct. Owing to the dynamic nature of the Internet, however, we cannot guarantee that all of these addresses will remain correct.

This series is for my father, Ron Chapman, with gratitude. – Garry Chapman
This series is dedicated to the memory of Jean and Alex Ross, as well as my immediate family of Sue, Hannah and Jessica, my parents, Jim and Val, and my brother Leigh. – Gary Hodges

Contents

Glossary Words

When a word is printed in **bold**, you can look up its meaning in the Glossary on page 31.

What Is a World Commodity?

A commodity is any product for which someone is willing to pay money. A world commodity is a product that is traded across the world.

The World's Most Widely Traded Commodities

Many of the world's most widely traded commodities are **agricultural** products, such as coffee, sugar, and wheat, or **natural resources**, such as coal, iron ore, and oil. These commodities are produced in large amounts by people around the world.

Coal, coffee, iron ore, oil, sugar, and wheat are important commodities traded around the world.

Commodities and the World's Economy

Whenever the world's **demand** for a commodity increases or decreases, the price of this commodity goes up or down by the same amount everywhere. Prices usually vary from day to day. The daily trade in world commodities plays a key role in the state of the world's **economy**.

MORE ABOUT...
The Quality of Commodities

When people, businesses, or countries buy a commodity, they assume that its quality will be consistent. Oil is an example of a commodity. When people trade in oil, all barrels of oil are considered to be of the same quality regardless of where they come from.

Coal Is a Commodity

Coal is a natural resource. It is the world's largest energy source for the generation of electricity. Coal is also used in the production of steel, cement, chemicals, plastics, and fuel.

A Fossil Fuel

Coal is a fossil fuel, composed mainly of carbon, hydrogen, and oxygen. Fossil fuels are used in the generation of electricity. Fossil fuels were formed over millions of years, when the remains of plants and animals became trapped under layers of **sediment**. Eventually, high levels of heat and pressure transformed the remains into fossil fuels.

The Characteristics of Coal

Coal is a **combustible** rock. Lignite, or brown coal, is usually used to generate power. Anthracite, a hard, glossy form of black coal, is used mainly for heating.

MORE ABOUT...
The Properties of Coal

Coal changes as it matures from its softest form, peat, to its hardest form, anthracite. The degree of change that coal undergoes determines its physical and chemical properties. Softer coals have higher moisture levels, lower carbon levels, and lower energy content than harder coals.

In some parts of China, bricks of coal are used for heating and cooking.

Where Is Coal Found and Where Is It Used?

Coal is mined commercially in more than 70 countries. There is still enough coal in reserve to last at least 160 years at the current rate of use.

United States

The United States has the world's largest coal reserves. It produces about 20 percent of the coal mined throughout the world each year. It also uses most of the coal it produces to generate electricity. Among the most important coal-mining regions in the United States are Illinois, Montana, West Virginia, and Wyoming.

COMMODITY FACT!

It has been predicted that China will increase coal production during the first 25 years of this century, contributing to an increase in global production. There are currently more than 20,000 coal-fired power plants in China.

THE WORLD'S MAJOR PRODUCERS OF COAL (2008)

Country	Amount of Coal Produced
China	3,037 tons (2,761 t)
United States	1,108 tons (1,007 t)
India	539 tons (490 t)
Australia	358 tons (325 t)
Russia	272 tons (247 t)

China

China also has large reserves of coal. It produces more coal each year than any other country, accounting for almost 40 percent of the world's annual production. Although it uses much of its coal to support its massive population, China is still one of the world's largest **exporters** of coal. Its coal industry employs more than 5 million people.

Australia

Australia has about 8 percent of the world's known coal reserves and is the world's largest exporter of coal. About three-quarters of all coal mined in Australia is exported, mainly to Asia. Coal is a major source of income for the country. Much of Australia's export coal is mined in the Hunter Valley, New South Wales, and shipped out of Newcastle, the world's busiest coal port.

Advanced technology at the port of Newcastle, Australia, helps load up to 11,550 tons (10,500 t) of coal per hour.

Europe

Coal production in Europe has declined in recent times. One reason for this is concern about the release of **greenhouse gases**, which result from the burning of coal. Russia and Germany, however, still have thriving coal industries. Russia's coal reserves are among the world's largest, particularly in remote parts of Siberia, beyond the Ural Mountains. Germany still produces more brown coal than any other country.

Asia—A Growing Market

The largest market for coal is Asia, which consumes more than half of the world's coal. This market is growing as India and China continue to develop their industries.

MORE ABOUT...
Coal Mining in Europe

The United Kingdom once had a booming coal industry in the north, but most of its coal mines were closed by the government in the 1980s. Cheaper **imported** coal and natural gas replaced British coal as energy sources.

Timeline: The History of Coal

Coal has been used as a source of heat and fuel for a very long time. The earliest evidence of coal use dates back more than 4,000 years, but it was not until the Han Dynasty in China that coal was used as a fuel.

206 B.C.
Coal is first used for heating purposes during the Han Dynasty in China.

A.D. 200
The Romans extract coal from surface coal fields across England and Wales and use it as a source of fuel in their iron factories.

1642
Coke, made from coal, is used to roast a grain called malt in Derbyshire, England. Wood as a fuel had become scarce, and coal could not be used in cooking because of its fumes, so coke was used instead.

about 1800
Coal becomes the main source of energy for industries. Powerful coal-fired steam trains and ships are used to transport goods. International trade booms. The introduction of safety lamps and steam-driven, air-circulation fans make mining safer.

206 B.C.

about 1350
In North America, the Aztecs use coal as a fuel for heating and cooking purposes.

about 1780
Large-scale, deep-shaft coal mining begins in the United Kingdom. **Colonists** discover coal deposits in North America.

about 1880
Efficient coal-cutting machines replace picks and shovels in mines.

1770s
The United Kingdom sees the start of the Industrial Revolution, a period of time when manufacturing by machines in factories grew in importance and scale. Coal is used to fuel the steam engines that power the machines. Northern England is dotted with coal mines.

1888
The Miners' Federation of Great Britain is one of several powerful trade unions formed to campaign against dangerous working conditions and low pay.

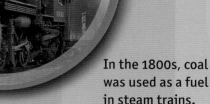

In the 1800s, coal was used as a fuel in steam trains.

Miners' strikes, such as this one in the 1920s, presented a way for miners to get better working conditions and wages.

1970s
Environmental issues related to coal mining, such as the destruction of land, air pollution, and **global warming**, gain more prominence.

1910
M. King Hubbert notes that coal production in the United States has grown at a steady rate of 6.6 per cent per year since 1850, but this rate is starting to level off and decline.

2000
Technology that helps to capture and store carbon dioxide, a greenhouse gas emitted by coal-fired power plants, is used for the first time. A site in Weyburn, Canada, stores carbon dioxide from a coal-fired gas plant in North Dakota.

1997
The Kyoto Protocol is adopted by many countries, imposing limits on the release of damaging greenhouse gases, most of which come from industries burning coal.

A.D. 2010

1960s
Cheaper and more efficient energy sources, such as oil and natural gas, begin to replace coal in homes, factories, and transportation.

1984
British miners go on strike between 1984 and 1985 against proposed mine closures. The strike fails, many mines are closed, and the industry disappears almost completely in the United Kingdom.

2010
Coal remains an important energy source, but its use is often limited to the production of electricity and steel. It faces competition from **renewable energy** and **biofuels**.

1968
Seventy-eight miners are killed during an explosion at a coal mine in Farmington, West Virginia, in the United States. The accident leads to the introduction of new laws in the United States aimed at protecting miners.

Coal-fired power plants must find ways to limit the emission of greenhouse gases, such as carbon dioxide.

How Is Coal Mined?

Coal is found in underground deposits known as seams. Coal seams are formed between layers, or strata, of harder rock. There are several ways to extract the seams from the rock.

Exploration

Exploration teams survey areas that are likely to contain coal. Engineers extract rock samples and **geologists** examine them. A new coal mine will be opened only if there is enough high-quality coal present for the mine to be profitable.

Selecting the Mining Method

The mining method is selected based on how deep the coal seams are. Seams less than 180 feet (55 m) below the ground are surface mined. This method recovers the greatest amount of coal from the ground as miners can more easily access all seams. Below 295 ft (90 m), seams are deep mined. About 60 percent of the world's coal mines are deep mines. Seams which lie between these two depths may be mined by either method. Geologists examine data to determine which method to use. Both methods can be carried out in two ways.

Surface Mining

Deep Mining

10

Strip Mining

The soil is removed in a long strip and deposited nearby. When all the coal has been mined from the strip, the soil is replaced and a new strip alongside it is removed.

Mountaintop and Contour Mining

If a coal seam lies close to a hilltop or ridge, the peak is removed to expose the coal, and the rock and soil are placed in nearby valleys. On sloping **terrain**, contours are cut into the side of the hill.

Room and Pillar Mining

Miners or equipment progress horizontally along a coal seam, removing much of it but leaving strong pillars of coal standing to support the roof. When the end of the seam is reached, the miners retreat, collapsing the pillars and removing the remaining coal as they go.

Longwall Mining

A machine known as a longwall shearer moves back and forth over the surface of the coal seam, scraping off pieces of coal as it moves. The coal falls onto a conveyor and is carried away. The shearer supports the roof of the mine as it progresses. When the shearer has passed, the roof collapses behind it.

Generating Electricity and Making Steel from Coal

Electricity and steel are important parts of our daily lives. Coal is used to generate electricity. Coke, a substance made from coal, is essential to the production of steel.

Generating Electricity From Coal

Power plants need a lot of coal every day to generate electricity. The coal may be transported to a nearby power plant by conveyor belt or carried farther by truck, train, barge, or ship.

Coal Is Burned

The coal is crushed until it becomes a powder. Jets of air blow the coal powder into a furnace, where it burns at high temperatures. Water circulating through pipes near the furnace is heated and changes into steam at around 1,004°F (540°C).

Steam Spins the Turbines

The steam rapidly spins large **turbines**, which turn a generator. A high-speed rotor spinning inside the generator creates electricity.

Transferring Electricity

The electricity flows to transformers, which increase its **voltage** before transmitting it to the power grid for distribution to households and industries.

Flue-Gas Emissions

Coal burned in power plants creates flue gas. Carbon dioxide and other emissions from flue gas contribute significantly to global warming. Many power plants now treat flue gas with steam to remove harmful pollutants before they are released into the air. They may also capture carbon dioxide from the flue gas emissions and store it safely.

Steel Production

Steel is a very useful metal. It is used in the construction of buildings and bridges, and in the production of vehicles, tools, and appliances. Coke, which is made from coal, is used to make steel.

Making Coke

When certain types of coal are baked at high temperatures in an airless furnace, they fuse with ash to form a hard substance known as coke.

Reduction in the Blast Furnace

Coke, iron ore, and limestone are fed into a blast furnace. Air is heated to about 2192°F (1200°C) and blown into the furnace. The coke burns, producing carbon monoxide and creating a chemical reaction. As the coke burns, removing the oxygen in the furnace, the iron ore becomes molten iron.

Steel Is Created

The molten iron is moved to another furnace, where steel scrap and limestone are added. Oxygen is blown over the mixture, removing any impurities and creating pure steel.

MORE ABOUT...

The Uses of Coal

Although coal is mainly used in the production of electricity and steel, it also plays a part in the manufacture of soap, medicine, cosmetics, shampoos, dyes, solvents, plastics, and nylon.

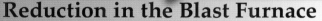

The Coal Trade

Coal is used to generate more than 40 percent of the world's electricity. The global coal trade comprises more than 70 producing countries and even more consuming countries.

The Early Coal Trade

Coal trading dates back to the 1700s in the United Kingdom and the United States. In the United Kingdom, steam engines were introduced during the Industrial Revolution. These engines required large amounts of coal to power machinery in factories and mills. Coal mines thrived in response to this new demand for fuel. In the United States, Americans were mining coal by the late 1770s to produce ammunition for the War of Independence.

COMMODITY FACT!

Coal is commonly transported across land by rail. Coal trains are among the heaviest in the world and can carry tens of thousands of tons of coal. They can also measure up to 1.2 miles (2 km) in length!

Coal trains are used in the coal trade to transport the commodity from where it is mined to where it is used.

Today, coal plays an important part in the creation of electricity and steel. This role and its relatively low cost compared to other energy sources have guaranteed a thriving global trade for the commodity.

Exchanges

An exchange is a place where commodities, such as coal, are bought and sold. At an exchange, coal is bought and sold in both the futures market and spot market.

The Futures Market

Trading in the futures market involves buying and selling contracts that are set in the future. Buyers and sellers agree on a price, which will be paid when the coal is delivered at a date in the future.

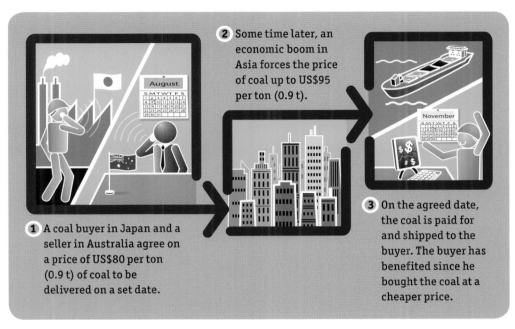

② Some time later, an economic boom in Asia forces the price of coal up to US$95 per ton (0.9 t).

① A coal buyer in Japan and a seller in Australia agree on a price of US$80 per ton (0.9 t) of coal to be delivered on a set date.

③ On the agreed date, the coal is paid for and shipped to the buyer. The buyer has benefited since he bought the coal at a cheaper price.

The futures trading of coal takes place in three main stages. The coal buyer is agreeing to buy coal at a future date for a set price.

The Spot Market

In the spot market, buyers and sellers agree on a price for the immediate exchange of goods. This means coal is delivered to the buyer as soon as it is purchased. Once the price is paid, the coal is transported from the mine to the place where it will be used, such as a power plant or steelworks.

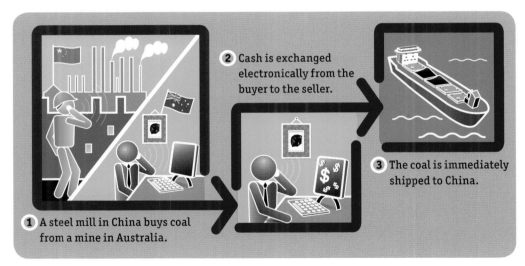

② Cash is exchanged electronically from the buyer to the seller.

① A steel mill in China buys coal from a mine in Australia.

③ The coal is immediately shipped to China.

The spot trading of coal is a simple transaction between a coal mining company and a steel mill that takes place in three main stages.

Supply and Demand

The coal trade is determined by **supply** and demand. When consumers are eager to buy the commodity, the demand for coal increases. Consumers rely on producers to supply it.

Factors Affecting Supply

There are many factors affecting the supply of coal.

- Finding new sources of coal will mean more coal can be mined.
- The availability of technology and labor will affect whether coal can be successfully mined.
- The transportation system in coal-mining countries determines whether coal can reach its export markets.

Factors Affecting Demand

Similarly, there are many factors affecting the demand for coal.

- Coal-consuming countries might import less coal if the world price rises.
- The demand for electricity will affect the demand for fuels, such as coal.
- The use of alternative sources of energy, such as wind energy and solar energy, will reduce the demand for fossil fuels, such as coal.

THE WORLD'S TOP EXPORTERS AND IMPORTERS OF COAL (2008)

Exporter	Amount of Coal Exported	Importer	Amount of Coal Imported
Australia	277 tons (252 t)	Japan	205 tons (186 t)
Indonesia	223 tons (203 t)	South Korea	110 tons (100 t)
Russia	111 tons (101 t)	Taiwan	73 tons (66 t)
Colombia	81 tons (74 t)	India	66 tons (60 t)
United States	81 tons (74 t)	China	51 tons (46 t)

Price Variations

When the global demand for coal is greater than its supply, the price of coal increases. In the same way, when the supply of coal is greater than the demand for it, the world coal price falls. Changes in the cost of producing coal can also affect the price of the commodity.

THE RISE AND FALL OF THE WORLD PRICE OF COAL

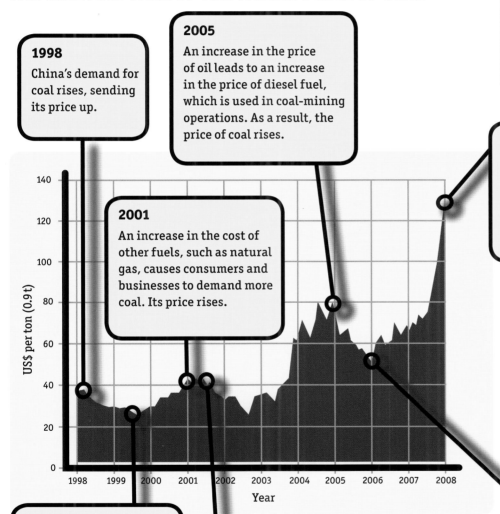

1998
China's demand for coal rises, sending its price up.

2005
An increase in the price of oil leads to an increase in the price of diesel fuel, which is used in coal-mining operations. As a result, the price of coal rises.

2001
An increase in the cost of other fuels, such as natural gas, causes consumers and businesses to demand more coal. Its price rises.

2008
A high demand for coal in China, to accommodate its massive industrialization needs, places pressure on coal supplies. The price of coal rises.

The world price of coal experiences highs and lows over time. Events around the world influence the supply of and demand for the commodity, which changes the price.

1999–2000
A global economic slowdown causes a dip in coal trading. The price of coal falls.

2001–2002
Following the September 11, 2001 terrorist attacks in the United States, a period of global uncertainty results in lower levels of trade. This leads to a fall in the price of coal.

2006
Decreasing demand for coal from Asia results in an oversupply in the coal market, pushing its price down.

17

Codes of Practice

Codes of practice govern the way most commodities are traded internationally. The purpose of these codes is to ensure that commodities are fairly priced and traded. Trading partners negotiate the conditions of a fair trade, the price to be paid and the amount of coal to be shipped.

Leading Coal Exchanges

Coal is traded on the NYMEX in units equal to 1,550 tons (1,406 t).

The New York Mercantile Exchange (NYMEX) and the Intercontinental Exchange (ICE) are leading coal exchanges. Both set their own **regulations** for the trading of coal.

Domestic Regulation of the Coal Industry

In some coal-producing countries, domestic regulations control the mining, processing and transportation of coal. In the United States, for example, the *Surface Mining Control and Reclamation Act* was introduced in 1977 to set the conditions under which surface mining could occur. Domestic regulations aim to protect the interests of one or more groups. These regulations may support coal-mining communities, look after the environment, or ensure that fuel for electricity generation reaches power plants.

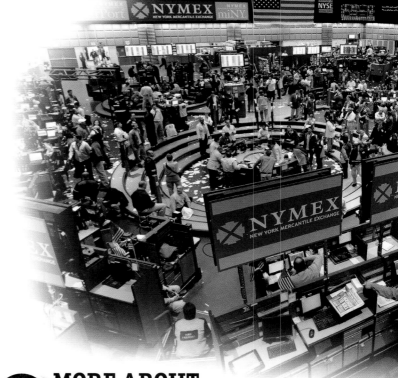

MORE ABOUT...

The *Surface Mining Control and Reclamation Act*

The *Surface Mining Control and Reclamation Act* in the United States governs the way coal-mining companies care for the environment during and after mining. President Gerald Ford had rejected this act in the mid-1970s because he feared it would harm the coal industry. However, his successor, President Jimmy Carter, believed it was necessary and made it law.

World Coal Institute

The World Coal Institute (WCI) was established in 1985. It is a nonprofit, nongovernmental organization. Many of the world's key coal-producing companies are members. The WCI encourages its members to adopt uniform guidelines on the production and trading of coal. It also provides information about coal to decision makers, educators, and the public.

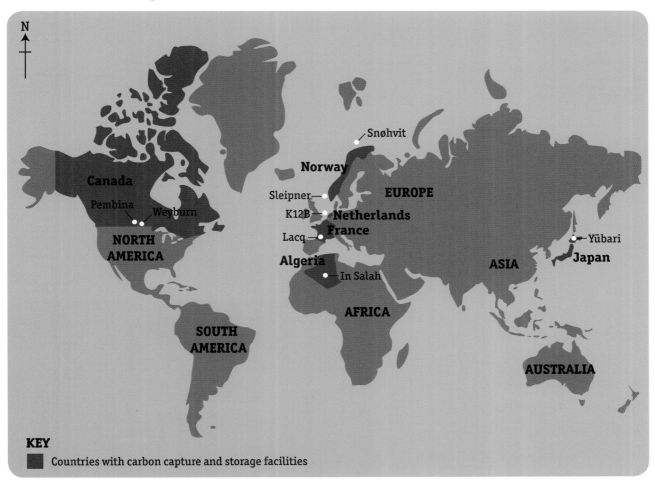

KEY
Countries with carbon capture and storage facilities

Statement of Commitment

The WCI's statement of commitment makes a number of important recommendations. It asks coal producers to:

- pay attention to **sustainable** development
- take steps to restrict greenhouse gas emissions
- install clean coal technologies
- implement safe mining and business practices

A number of countries around the world have carbon capture and storage facilities either on land or at sea. Carbon capture and storage, also known as carbon sequestration, is a clean coal technology that is recommended by the WCI.

International Politics and Coal

The world's leading trading countries rely on coal-generated electricity to power their industries. However, the greenhouse gas emissions produced by coal-fired power plants contribute to climate change and Earth's rising temperature. The use of coal has become an issue of political debate as the world's governments look for ways to solve this problem.

United Nations Climate Change Conference

World leaders met in Copenhagen, Denmark, in December 2009, for the United Nations Climate Change Conference. One aim of the conference was for the leaders to reach agreement on a number of measures which would limit the amount of greenhouse gases emitted in their countries. This would be achieved by setting targets for each **developed country** to reduce its emissions by 2020.

Different Views

Some leaders wanted a commitment to achieving significant reductions in greenhouse gas emissions. They argued that if this did not happen, the impact on their countries could be disastrous. For example, Pacific Islanders fear that climate change will cause the polar ice caps and glaciers to melt. This could raise sea levels and flood their low-lying countries. Some of the larger developed countries were reluctant to agree to significant reductions. They were concerned that the impact of such emissions targets could be harmful to their industries and economies.

The management of carbon dioxide emissions from coal-fired power plants was one of the main issues discussed at the 2009 United Nations Climate Change Conference.

The Copenhagen Accord

In a statement called the Copenhagen Accord, world leaders stated their intent to continue to tackle the key issues of climate change. The accord recognized that:

- the amount of greenhouse gases in the atmosphere should be stabilized at safe levels
- the rise in the world's temperature should be limited to below 35.6°F (2°C)
- countries should work together to achieve the peak of world and domestic emissions as soon as possible
- **developing countries**, such as China and India, will take longer than developed countries, such as the United States, to achieve these goals and should be supported in their efforts to reduce emissions

Activists outside the 2009 United Nations Climate Change Conference protested about the way in which world leaders were handling this important issue.

The Use of Coal in China

The environmental organization Greenpeace claims that in China, 80 percent of carbon dioxide emissions and 85 percent of sulfur dioxide emissions result from the burning of coal. If China is to support the Copenhagen Accord, it must either install clean coal technologies in its thousands of power plants or find alternative cleaner sources of energy.

Environmental Issues and Coal

Ever since its rise to prominence during the Industrial Revolution, coal has been linked to widespread environmental damage. Most recently it has been linked to global warming and climate change.

Greenhouse Gases

Damaging greenhouse gases, which result from the burning of coal, are released by many coal-fired power plants. These emissions are carried high into the atmosphere, where they trap radiation from the sun and contribute to global warming. Global warming may result in the melting of polar ice caps, a rise in sea levels, and an increase in extreme weather events. These events are linked to climate change and their impacts may be felt by all living things.

Clean coal technology was tested at a coal-fired power plant at Longanet, Scotland in 2009. The process removes carbon dioxide and turns it into a liquid, which is then stored underground.

COMMODITY FACT!

The Union of Concerned Scientists estimates that in an average year, a 500-megawatt coal-fired power plant generates:

- 3.7 million tons (3.3 million t) of carbon dioxide
- 10,000 tons (9,000 t) of sulfur dioxide
- 10,200 tons (9,180 t) of nitrogen oxide

Clean Coal Technologies

Clean coal technologies are being developed to help minimize the harmful emissions from power plants. However, many existing power plants have yet to implement them because of the high costs involved.

Destruction of the Landscape

Coal mining has had a negative impact on the landscape. Forests have been cleared to make way for mine sites, causing soil erosion, disturbing wildlife habitats, and reducing plant species. Today, coal-mining companies often employ environmentalists to ensure that the impact of mining operations on the landscape is reduced.

Water Contamination

When coal is mined, the process can disturb both surface and underground water systems. Toxic substances may flow from the mine into the water, causing contamination. Coal-mining companies often prevent contamination by transferring wastewater to special ponds. The water is left in the pond long enough for sediment to settle. When the water is clear, it is removed. The sediment at the bottom of the pond is then safely disposed of.

"If we can develop the technology to capture the carbon pollution released by coal, it can create jobs and provide energy well into the future. So today I'm announcing a Carbon Capture and Storage Task Force that will be charged with the goal of figuring out how we can deploy affordable clean coal technology on a widespread scale within 10 years."

United States President Barack Obama, 2010
(Source: www.whitehouse.gov/the-press-office/remarks-president-and-vice-president-meeting-with-governors-energy-policy)

One way to reduce the impact of coal mining on the landscape is to reclaim land that has been mined. This former strip mine in West Virginia is being sprayed with grass seed to promote the growth of new grass.

Social Issues and Coal

Many people in coal-mining communities rely on the jobs and income that the industry provides.

The Impact of Mine Closures

When mines close, workers are often left without jobs and the benefits that accompany employment. In the past, this led to increases in crime, depression, and alcoholism in former coal-mining communities. Houses in such communities dropped in value and businesses struggled. Today, many coal-mining companies plan ahead to ensure that workers are supported when a mine closes by retraining them or helping them find new jobs in other mines. Mining communities are also encouraged to develop other industries so that people can continue living in the area and have employment opportunities when the mine closes.

Mining accidents, such as the one pictured below in Wales in 1966, can devastate entire towns.

Safety Issues in Mines

In the past, mining accidents were caused by poor mine construction, lack of adequate equipment, or the absence of safety regulations. Shifting beams or water leaks led to underground mine collapses. The lack of proper masks meant miners often breathed in poisonous gases or harmful coal dust. A mining accident resulting in the loss of many lives could rob a community of its husbands and sons. Today, improved mining technology and safety equipment help make coal mining a much safer job than it once was.

MORE ABOUT...
Mining Accidents

The people of the Welsh village of Aberfan relied heavily on the coal industry. One day in 1966, tragedy struck. Heavy rain caused a landslide in a huge pile of mining waste. More than 5.3 million cubic feet (150,000 cubic m) of rock broke away and slid downhill, smashing into the village and killing 144 villagers, including 116 children.

Trade Unions

Trade unions are organized groups of workers from a particular trade, led by their own elected representatives. Union leaders negotiate with mining companies for better wages and working conditions for their members. Failure to reach a compromise may result in union members going on strike.

United Kingdom Miners' Strike (1984–1985)

When the British government announced that it would close 20 mines at a cost of almost 20,000 jobs in 1984, the National Union of Mineworkers began a year-long strike. The strike brought much hardship to the miners and their families. Eventually, the union gave in to the government, and the strike was defeated. The mines were closed, the miners lost their jobs, and the union never regained its power.

Between 1984 and 1985, coal miners and their families protested against the closure of mines in the United Kingdom.

Is the Coal Industry Sustainable?

To sustain something is to keep it going for a very long time. There are two main aspects to keeping the coal industry sustainable: maintaining the demand for coal and protecting the environment from the effects of mining and burning coal.

A Nonrenewable Energy Source

Coal is readily available in many countries and will be for more than 100 years. However, coal is a **nonrenewable energy** source, and a time will come when it can no longer be relied on. It may be possible to extend the lifespan of the world's coal reserves by finding ways to use less coal now. The easiest way to do this is to limit the electricity we use. We can turn lights and appliances off when they are not in use, reduce the use of heaters and air conditioners, and use energy-efficient light bulbs.

If coal's harmful emissions are not controlled, consumers might choose cleaner energy sources, such as wind power.

COMMODITY FACT!

Coal-fired power plants built in the 2000s emit 40 percent less carbon dioxide than those built in the 1900s.

Alternative Energy Sources

If consumers grow dissatisfied with emission levels from coal-fired power plants, they may resort to alternative energy sources long before the world's coal reserves are exhausted. Wind, water, and solar energies are examples of alternative energy. They are also renewable energy sources and unlikely to harm the environment. The knowledge and technology to generate power from these sources already exists but can be costly.

Protecting the Environment

Mining coal and burning it to create electricity can have a significant impact on the environment. If we switch to using cleaner alternative-energy sources and adopt habits which help the environment, the coal that remains will last longer. Coal can then be used only when necessary and when other options are not available. However, the way coal is used must still be changed to reduce emissions at their source—the power plant.

Clean Coal Technologies

Recently introduced clean coal technologies attempt to significantly reduce the emissions that contribute to global warming. Many of the harmful gases found in coal smoke can be safely removed. The challenge now is to improve technologies that will capture and safely store the gases produced by burning coal, particularly carbon dioxide. However, this technology is very costly and has yet to be implemented widely.

The impact of coal mining on the environment can be reduced if creative solutions can be found. This old coal mine in West Virginia is now used as a golf course.

The Future of the Coal Industry

The coal industry faces significant challenges in the near future. Although coal reserves may last more than 100 years, greenhouse gas emissions must be reduced before the world looks elsewhere for its energy sources.

Reducing Greenhouse Gas Emissions

Reducing greenhouse gas emissions is likely to be a costly process. Power companies may have to absorb the high costs of installing clean coal technologies. Governments may be able to reduce such costs by providing tax incentives or subsidies for businesses that adopt these technologies and other measures.

Emissions Trading

During the late 1990s, many countries adopted the Kyoto Protocol, which meant they agreed to reduce their greenhouse gas emissions. Countries that signed the protocol agreed to limit their emissions to a certain amount. Governments in these countries award **carbon credits** to companies that need them. These credits are used up when a company reaches its emissions limit. If more carbon credits are needed, the company can buy them from another company that does not need as many credits. The penalty for emitting greenhouse gases without credit is a heavy fine.

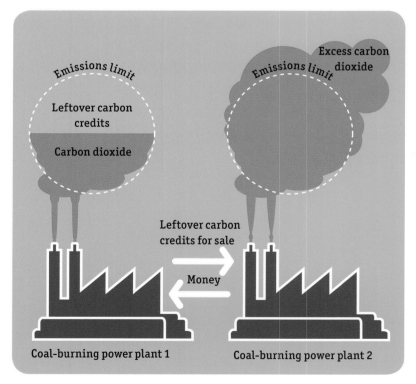

Under the Kyoto Protocol, the owners of coal-fired power plants that emit high levels of greenhouse gases can buy carbon credits from the owners of power plants with lower emissions.

Carbon Sequestration

Carbon sequestration offers a solution to reducing greenhouse gas emissions by storing carbon dioxide safely underground or deep in the ocean, rather than releasing it into the atmosphere. The challenge is to develop the sequestration process to the point where it can safely store a significant proportion of the carbon dioxide generated by the world's power plants long into the future.

MORE ABOUT...
Carbon Sequestration

The Sleipner Project is the world's first large-scale carbon sequestration project. Statoil, a Norwegian energy company, has been injecting carbon dioxide deep into the floor of the North Sea since the mid-1990s. In return for this environmentally friendly carbon disposal initiative, the company receives tax benefits from the Norwegian government.

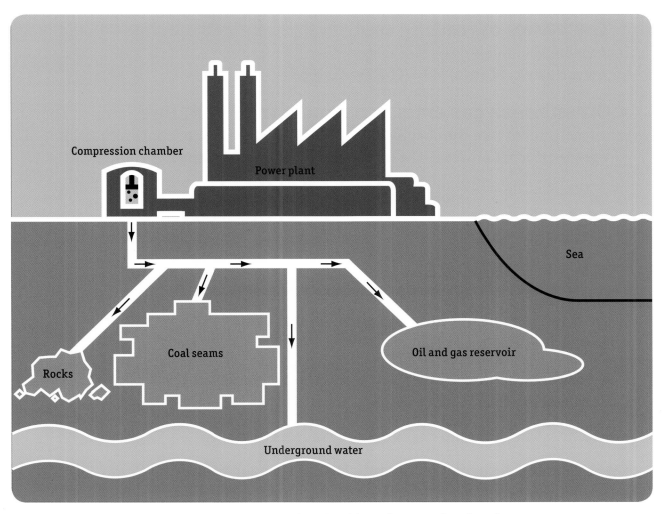

Carbon sequestration is a process that stores carbon dioxide underground or deep in the ocean. This illustration shows how emissions from a power plant are directed into a compression chamber and then transported by pipes into suitable storage sites on land. This could be a rock formation, coal seams, underground water storages, or an oil and gas reservoir.

Find Out More

Web Sites for Further Information

- ### The formation of coal
  Learn more about the different stages in the formation of coal.
  http://geology.com/rocks/coal.shtml

- ### Mining coal
  Learn more about the different methods of mining coal.
  www.worldcoal.org/coal/coal-mining/

- ### The basics of trading coal
  Learn more about how coal trading works.
  www.clean-coal.info/pubs/CoalTrading.pdf

- ### Greenhouse gas emissions and climate change
  Learn more about how the coal industry is tackling the issue of climate change.
  www.worldcoal.org/coal-the-environment/climate-change/

Focus Questions

These questions might help you think about some of the issues raised in this book.

- Do you think the benefits of clean coal technologies justify the additional expense?

- What are some of the alternative energy sources to coal?

- Will clean coal technologies be available soon enough to stop global warming?

- Can the choices we make about the use of coal-based products make a difference to global warming?

Glossary

activists	workers for political or social change
agricultural	related to farming or used for farming
biofuels	fuels that are made from living things or their waste
carbon credits	units that measure the amount of carbon dioxide emitted into the atmosphere
colonists	people who have settled and are governing a country that did not originally belong to them
combustible	able to burn easily
demand	the amount of a product consumers want to buy
developed country	a country that is very industrialized
developing countries	countries in the early stages of becoming industrialized
domestic	relating to a person's own country
economy	a system that organizes the production, distribution, and exchange of goods and services, as well as incomes
exporters	countries which sell or send a product to another country
geologists	people who study the rocks and other substances that make up Earth's surface
global warming	an increase in the world temperature caused by greenhouse gases in the atmosphere
greenhouse gases	gases found in the air that trap heat around Earth and cause higher temperatures
imported	bought or brought in from another country
natural resources	the naturally occurring, useful wealth of a region or country, such as land, forests, coal, oil, gas, and water
nonrenewable energy	energy from a source that will run out
regulations	rules
renewable energy	energy from a source that will not run out
sediment	very tiny pieces of solid matter that settle at the bottom of a liquid
supply	the amount of a product that producers are able to sell
surplus	an amount which is more than is needed
sustainable	developed or designed so that the production of a commodity can continue for a long time
terrain	an area of land and its natural features
turbines	machines with blades that turn when a liquid or gas flows through them
voltage	the force of an electric current, which is measured in volts

Index